To Stephanie and her grandmother,
without whose help I wouldn't have written this book

Grandma Comes to Stay copyright ©Frances Lincoln Limited 2009
Text and photographs copyright ©Ifeoma Onyefulu 2009

First published in Great Britain in 2009 and the USA in 2010 by
Frances Lincoln Children's Books,
74-77 White Lion Street,
London N1 9PF
www.franceslincoln.com

This paperback edition first published in Great Britain and in the USA in 2015

A CIP catalogue record for this book is available from the British Library.

ISBN: 978-1-84780-251-4

Printed in China

1 3 5 7 9 8 6 4 2

IFEOMA ONYEFULU was brought up in a traditional village in Eastern Nigeria. Her highly acclaimed children's books are renowned for countering negative images of Africa by celebrating both its traditional village life and its urban life. *A is for Africa*, her first book, has become a classic title in the genre of cultural diversity and was praised by Publishers Weekly for its 'incisive view of her country's rich heritage'. Ifeoma has twice won the Children's Africana Book Award: Best Book for Young Children in the USA, with *Here Comes Our Bride* and *Ikenna Goes to Nigeria*. *Deron Goes to Nursery School* was shortlisted for the prestigious English 4-11 Awards. Ifeoma lives in London with her two sons.

www.ifeomaonyefulu.co.uk
www.ifeomaonyefulu.co.uk/mytravels/

GRANDMA
COMES TO STAY

Ifeoma Onyefulu

F

FRANCES LINCOLN
CHILDREN'S BOOKS

This is Stephanie.

Stephanie is three.

Stephanie lives here with her mum,
dad and big sister, Mary.

Stephanie's friends have come to play
but all Stephanie wants to do is

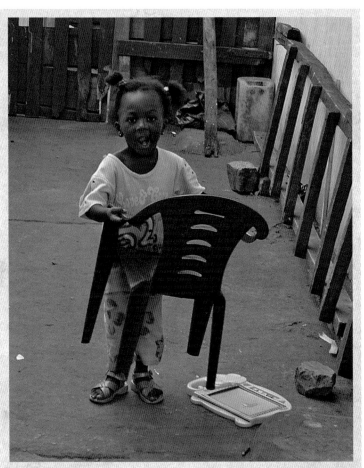

sweep the floor...   arrange the chairs...

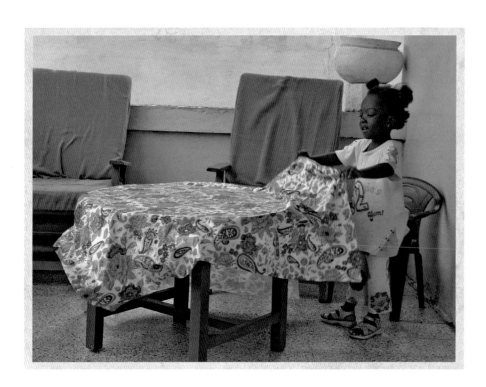

tidy up...

help with the shopping
at Kaneshie market...

and help Mummy with the cooking.

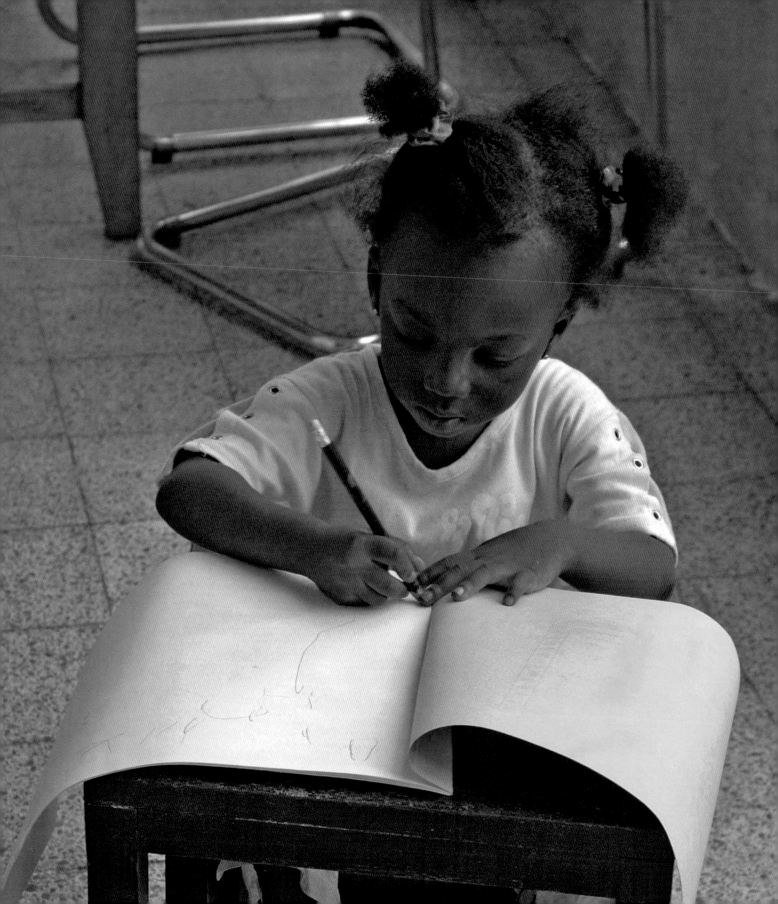

Then Stephanie sits down
and does a lovely drawing...
because someone special
is coming to stay.

Grandma!

Grandma says "Thank you" to Stephanie for working so hard, and gives her a box of pencils.

Then Grandma, Stephanie, Mary, Mum and Dad sit down at the table for a meal.

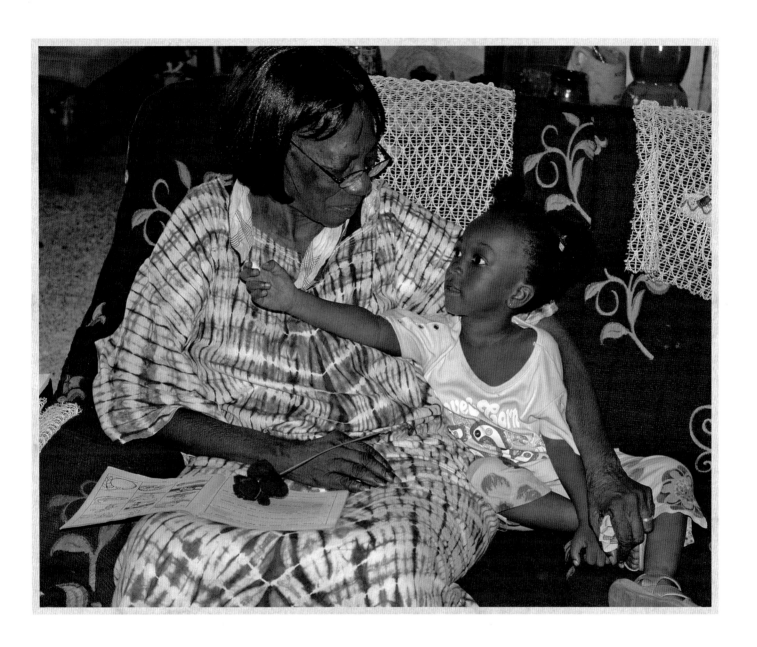

Later, Grandma reads Stephanie her favourite book.

Next morning, Grandma shows
Stephanie how to tie a wrapper...

and a head-dress.

Then Stephanie shows Grandma
how to kick a ball...

ride a bike...

use a counting book...

play with dolls...

do the ironing...

and play the drum.

In the afternoon, Grandma takes Stephanie
and Mary to see real-life drummers and dancers
at Osu Homowo festival.

And at bedtime, Grandma tells Stephanie
a wonderful story about a magic drum.

Next morning, it's time for Grandma to say goodbye. "Come back soon, Grandma!" say Stephanie and Mary.

COLLECT ALL THE BOOKS IN IFEOMA ONYEFULU'S ACCLAIMED FIRST EXPERIENCES SERIES:

Deron Goes to Nursery School

978-1-84780-252-1

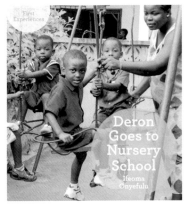

Grandma Comes to Stay

978-1-84780-251-4

Omer's Favourite Place

978-1-84780-129-6

New Shoes for Helen

978-1-84780-128-9

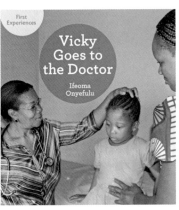

Vicky Goes to the Doctor

978-1-84780-363-4

Ife's First Haircut

978-1-84780-364-1

Frances Lincoln titles are available from all good bookshops.
You can also buy books and find out more about your favourite titles, authors
and illustrators on our website: www.franceslincoln.com